THE ART OF
Quilting
MACHINE TECHNIQUES & DESIGNS

JUDY WOODWORTH

American Quilter's Society
www.AmericanQuilter.com

The American Quilter's Society or AQS is dedicated to quilting excellence. AQS promotes the triumphs of today's quilter, while remaining dedicated to the quilting tradition. AQS believes in the promotion of this art and craft through AQS Publishing and AQS QuiltWeek®.

CONTENT EDITOR: CAITLIN M. TETREV
ILLUSTRATIONS: LYNDA SMITH
GRAPHIC DESIGN: ELAINE WILSON
COVER DESIGN: MICHAEL BUCKINGHAM/SARAH BOZONE
QUILT PHOTOGRAPHY: CHARLES R. LYNCH
HOW-TO PHOTOGRAPHY: JUDY WOODWORTH
ASSISTANT EDITOR: ADRIANA FITCH
DIRECTOR OF PUBLICATIONS: KIMBERLY HOLLAND TETREV

Additional copies of this book may be ordered from the American Quilter's Society, PO Box 3290, Paducah, KY 42002-3290, or online at www.ShopAQS.com.

Attention Photocopying Service: Please note the following—Publisher and author give permission to print pages 56, 69–93.

American Quilter's Society
www.AmericanQuilter.com

Library of Congress Cataloging-in-Publication Data

Names: Woodworth, Judy, author.
Title: The art of quilting : machine techniques & designs / By Judy Woodworth.
Description: Paducah, KY : American Quilter's Society, 2016.
Identifiers: LCCN 2015045569 | ISBN 9781604602814 (pbk.) | ISBN 9781604609264 (ebook)
Subjects: LCSH: Machine quilting. | Machine quilting--Patterns.
Classification: LCC TT835 .W65945 2016 | DDC 746.46--dc23
LC record available at http://lccn.loc.gov/2015045569

DEDICATION & APPRECIATION

My dedication and my appreciation always has to start with my Husband Bill (Woody) Woodworth. Without his encouragement I would never have written any books. For the last fifty years he has always believed in me. I hope everyone who reads this book can find a person who supports you in your endeavors, makes you believe in yourself, and gives you inspiration. I hope I can be the person to spark that flame for those who just need a loving push to try to be more creative.

My students have been wonderfully receptive to my kind of gentle but persuasive encouragement and instructions. They have given me so much kindness and they have even shared their own inspirations with me. It's always been a journey with my teaching, to reach out to every student, to pull out that glimmer of hope, that "I can do it attitude", and to be a catalyst for them to reach their goals.

The editors and staff at the American Quilter's Society believed in me, when in my mind the idea of writing a book was only for those famous quilters and not, at the time of my first book, an unknown like me. This is my third book with AQS and they are such professionals. I hope that if you have a kernel of an idea about writing a book that you'll pursue your dreams, even if you try and get rejected on a few of them. Keep trying!

Always thanks go to my quilting buddy and best friend, Mary Sue Suit.

Last I would like to thank the two County Fair Judges who gave me the worst critiques that almost made me stop quilting and taking photos. Little did they know that they would be such a factor in developing my quilting and in my study of art and composition.

TITLE PAGE: Easy Diamonds, detail. Full quilt on p. 30

BACKGROUND: Tuscany Memories, detail. Full quilt on p. 28

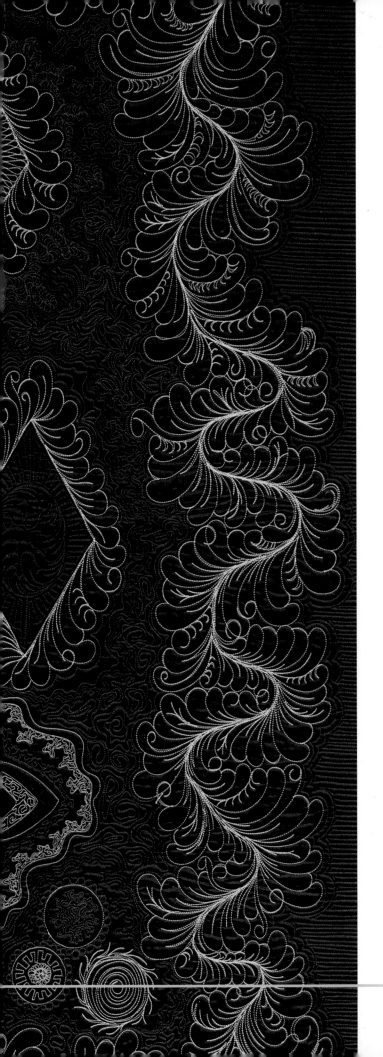

CONTENTS

LEFT: GLIDE QUILT, detail. Full quilt on p. 94.

INTRODUCTION

This book is a compilation of the things I have learned about quilting and designing over the last twenty years. Some of the knowledge is from working on quilts that have failed and from working on those that have succeeded. I've learned how composition and art design can really affect the strength of not only your quilting design but also the actual quilting. I'll give you tips on quilting techniques I've learned the hard way so you can avoid some of my earlier pitfalls. I'll share some things I've learned from judges, and I'll finish off with many samples of freemotion quilting and completed quilt designs. I guess you can call this book a medley of quilting ideas.

I've asked other quilters what inspires them, how, and

RIGHT: **EMERGING SPRING,** detail. Full quilt on p. 11.

where they emphasize their main focus. I've read probably over a hundred books, many I checked out from the library, so my knowledge of composition, design, and the study of art have come from many sources. Through all my questions and studies I have seen certain strong, central points of composition and art being utilized over and over. I tried and experimented with all these art theories and by trial and error I learned what I think works for quilting.

I have to begin with the County Fair Judges, whose stark criticism was the catalyst for my striving to learn everything I could about quilting and the world of art. I was a hobby photographer long before I became a quilter. The things I studied helped me become a more complete artist, in photography and quilting. My knowledge that I share with you is based on my personal experiences and years of reading and studying art.

My first quilt was made for my daughter as a wedding present. I was a sewer at the time, but knew nothing about making a quilt. I remember we picked out this beautiful flower fabric, which was just too pretty to cut up into tiny pieces. So I cut them into 12" squares only and put sashing all around the blocks. I chalk penciled a cable design from a stencil into the sashing and used my regular home sewing machine to machine quilt. When I was done I couldn't figure out how to quilt in all those flower squares. In the end, my daughter Angela and I decided against quilting them. We tied the quilt with green yarn

and I sewed on the binding by machine like you would a hem, it wasn't awful.

My daughter loved the quilt so much that she wanted us to enter it in the county fair. Back then we got to watch and listen to the judging. When the Judge got to mine she said, "This might make a good utility quilt…" with the word might having an implied question mark next to it, "but this quilt is not good enough for a ribbon. She mixed two techniques which is a big no-no and her binding is very bad."

I remember backing away from the other quilters and crying. On the way to the car I told my daughter I was never going to make another quilt, much less enter it into a quilt show. She put her arm around me and told me she loved the quilt and she would have it on her bed forever. Children are so good for a person's confidence.

The reason I share this story with you is for inspiration because in the years since that fair, I have won over a hundred major quilting awards. Right now you may think you are the worst quilter in the world or maybe you are just a beginner. All you need to be is willing to do some experimenting. What works for me, might not work for you (or it might).

You may wonder what made me start studying art and how it affects a quilt and the quilting. I can thank a second County Fair judge in the photography division for this. The Fair instruction book said to take a grouping of pictures of something that you enjoy. No other instructions were listed, including any composition requirements. I decided to take a grouping of photos of antiques, because I really enjoy antiquing. When my work was presented the Judge said "What was she thinking? She didn't use the three division composition rule." At that time I was a photographer, and I knew for a fact that there were many different types of composition. Rather than get upset at the judge for trying to impose rules not outlined in the fair instruction book, I decided to take that disappointment and turn it into a learning experience.

At the time I took the antiques photos, I had not studied composition and design. I think I looked at them through a quilter's eye though. When I looked at the antique silverware settings on the red table cloth in a horizontal composition, I was drawn to the contrast between the red and the silver (photo 1, p. 9).

I remembered thinking that it was well balanced and although there wasn't a strong central focus of any one item, the tarnished butter dish was the closest to a main focus item. By its very contrast to all the other silver ones which were shiny, this one was more subdued in color. If I was taking this picture again, I would have probably shifted the butter dish up and centered it more into the right bottom quarter section of the picture and pushed the other silverware slightly away from it to isolate it. Based on this, I'll share with you what I learned about on where to place the main focus in the design.

I loved the second photo for all the wonderful quilting patterns and textures on the glasses (photo 2, p. 9). The lines were topped by simple flowers that were different in contrast and height. The bottom portions of the glasses were divided by other lines in a different color. The beautiful colors of white, pink, and blue pastels were fabulous. The curly spiraling top to the glass holder was an amazing contrast of metal to glass and design. Could I have changed this horizontal composition so that the silver curling spiral was sitting more to the right and centered in the top right section? Yes. Would it have made it more of a main focus? Yes.

In my third photo, the white hat is the main focus item. Some people might argue that the lips that were drawn on the Styrofoam™ could be the focus. I believe the white hat really captures your attention, because of the darker wood background. These contrasts in light and dark are what we do in quilting to make a strong quilt (photo 3, p. 9).

The fourth photo is my favorite color combination in a very relaxing horizontal composition. You have the frosty green pastel and the almost true green Fostoria glasses. The little red flowers on the table cloth are almost the main focus just because it's the only place in the photo with this bold color. Red is the opposite on the color wheel of green. The colors really stand out from one another because they are not equal parts of green and red (photo 4, p. 9).

Photo 1

Photo 2

Photo 3

Photo 4

Photo 5

When I was studying composition, they said the dark colors would recede into the background. I have found in some photography that when there are only a few darker colors, because of the contrast, they can actually make your eye notice it first. So my number one thing for you to realize when you study art is just because it is the rule, doesn't mean you have to follow it. The final picture is a testament to that idea.

Instead of following the rule of thirds it follows a constellation or cluster composition. I felt the most emotion when I took this photo. I looked into that tub of random silverware and thought about all the hundreds of families that probably used these over many centuries. The sad silverware was just thrown in a big tub as if they had just been thrown away, as if they hadn't been touched by a family member every single day. To me it was like the people were also forgotten (photo 5).

Not everyone will understand your vision just remember it is your creation. Yes, hopefully you've capture the essence of what you were feeling in a photograph or a quilt, but maybe only you know the hidden meaning. Rejoice in your individuality.

EMERGING SPRING, 63" x 73". Designed and pieced by Mary Sue Suit,
Sidney, Nebraska. Quilted by the author.

TYPES OF COMPOSITION

There are so many composition designs that I can't show them all here. However, I can show you the ones I think quilters can use in their quilts whether you do traditional or art quilts.

Vertical Composition

My personal favorite is the vertical composition. Most bed quilts are vertical because they are made for a bed, although king size beds are sometimes square. Show quilts tend many times to be vertical because of the way they hang in a show and they are usually attention getters. Don't make a vertical composition just because you think it will look more dominant hanging in a show if it doesn't fit the mood of your design.

Fig. 1–1. Composition 1–Vertical

This vertical composition, Composition 1 represents strength and power (fig. 1–1). It generally makes quite a statement. In art quilts you will many times see tall trees, skyscrapers, light houses, large or life-sized people and dragons in a vertical composition. If you wanted a serene or peaceful setting or feeling you wouldn't want to use a vertical composition.

Horizontal Composition

When you want to depict a relaxing and peaceful setting, use a horizontal composition. I have seen pictures of tree trunks in a horizontal composition and it takes on a different feeling. In a way, it looks and feels calmer.

Fig. 1–2. Composition 2–Horizontal

Composition 2 is horizontal, but also has the three division composition in the body of the quilt. You'll see the foreground, the horizon, and the sky (fig. 1–2). These divisions do not have to be in equal portions.

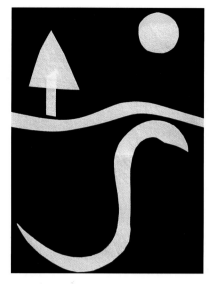

Fig. 1–3. Composition 3–Three Division, S Composition

Three Division, S Composition in a Vertical Composition

Many quilts have several different types of compositions in the body of the quilt. The S composition in Composition 3 represents the powerful river which is the main focus. In my opinion, this composition needs to be in a vertical composition to represent the vibrancy and strength of the powerful river. The river itself is not only an S composition, but it has a diagonal design and represents movement (fig. 1–3).

Diagonal Composition

Using diagonal composition you can bring out motion, tension, and force in your quilt. In a traditional quilt, using this composition gives off a lot more excitement and energy. For an art quilt, a crashing wave is going to use diagonal composition, which will allow your viewers to feel the movement of the wave. As it is in Composition 4 all the diagonally placed lines gives movement to the other shapes. Making it look as it everything is being blown around (fig. 1–4).

Fig. 1–4. Composition 4–Diagonal Composition

Framed and Spiral Composition

Many of our traditional quilts have borders and sashing which represent a framed composition. This means that the quilter has literally made a frame for the composition.

Fig. 1–5. Spirals in Summer Raindrops, spiral details. Full quilt on p. 15.

The Spiral composition is prevalent in many of my quilting designs. When I put spirals in my quilting, as in my quilt Spirals in Summer Raindrops, p. 15 and fig. 1–5, I use them in several sizes and shapes and distribute them throughout the quilt. If you will notice in Composition 5 the spirals at the bottom of the design are larger and bolder. There are three spirals grouped together at the bottom and a single spiral at the top (fig. 1–6). This weighs the design at the bottom as things would be in nature. A tree truck would be heavier at the bottom and the branches would be thinner at the top.

Grid Block Composition

Most of our traditional quilts are in a Grid Block composition. A photo or a quilt with a bird's eye view looking down at the plowed farm lands would be in a grid composition. In my house (Composition 6, fig. 1–7), I have left an opening at the left side so that the eye can travel into the design from the left and proceed to the right, as is the standard for English speaking people. For viewing art, I find this art standard also translates to a quilt. Expect viewers to look at your quilt from left to right.

Fig. 1–6. Composition 5–Framed and Spiral Composition in a vertical composition.

Fig. 1–7. Composition 6–Grid Block Composition.

SPIRALS IN SUMMER RAINDROPS, 38" x 51". Designed, pieced, and quilted by the author.

Fig. 1–8. Composition 7–Circular

Fig. 1–9. Composition 8–Radial Composition

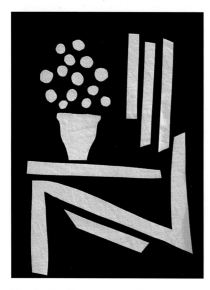

Fig. 1–10. Composition 9– Constellation and Z Composition

Circular Composition

Quilts that are circular by nature are generally in a square composition, although you may find some medallion quilts are circular. When the quilt is a circular design but isn't a symmetrical design, I will quilt it in a circle. I call this chasing the design. All the designs are going the same direction around the quilt.

You may have a design with lots of circles placed randomly in the body of the quilt with different shapes and sizes throughout the quilt top. It is asymmetrical. If there is a border around the whole outside quilt I will have the quilting patterns facing the same direction all the way around the border and back up to the top. I won't do a symmetrical quilting design around that border. If I had a symmetrical quilt, I would do the border designs symmetrically. With my quilting I try to incorporate circles in the quilting to support the circle theme, but sometimes I will put a square or straight line objects to give contrast. In Composition 7, the circles radiate out but in the middle is a solid shape giving the circles a point to radiate out from (fig. 1–8). Quilting is all about your vision.

Radiating Composition

Think of a radial tire that goes around in a circle. This is not a symmetrical composition and I would definitely quilt the design chasing around the circle (or border). It's best in a square composition to really show the radiation movement from its starting point to ending point (fig. 1–9).

Constellation and Z Composition

Remember when I took the picture of the silverware? This would have been a constellation composition. Have you ever seen pictures of marbles, or stones? This grouping is also a constellation composition. The flowers in Composition 9, represent the constellation (or cluster) composition (fig. 1–10).

The Z composition is not the shape of a quilt, but you will see the Z composition in the components of a design sometimes. It is an interesting design.

Symmetrical

Symmetrical composition does not have to be done in a square format, although it is one of my favorite quilting designs for a square. However, my friend Mary Sue Suit's quilts are almost always in a vertical composition, but they are symmetrical. THE ROSES BETWEEN FRIENDS quilt (p. 40) is a perfect example of Symmetrical composition.

If you look at this vertical composition in fig. 1–11a, compared to the horizontal composition in fig. 1–11b, the former looks more intimidating while the latter looks less aggressive.

FAIRY DUST, p. 18, is symmetrical and has a circular composition in the piecing. The center and second row embroidery is symmetrical, but the outside embroidered fairies are in a circular composition, all are radiating out the same way. There were such strong circular shapes to the quilting I decided to have the fairies chasing each other around in a circle. The feathers were neither symmetrical nor circular, but I wanted them to represent the fairy winds that were blowing randomly around that outer circular. It was just my interpretation, but all the Judges seemed to like what I had done. I won Best of Show, so again there are no absolute rules here.

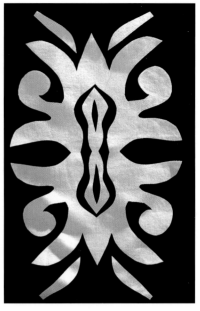

Fig. 1–11a. Composition 10–Symmetrical in a vertical composition.

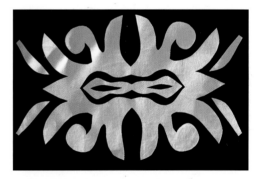

Fig. 1–11b. Composition 10b–Symmetrical in a horizontal composition.

FAIRY DUST, 60" x 60". Designed, pieced, and quilted by the author.

BASIC ART PRINCIPLES

Basic Principles and Elements of Art

This is the part where you probably want to squeeze your eyes closed and yell at me, "No, I don't want to learn this." How can knowing about the technicalities of art have anything to do with making a traditional quilt, you're wondering? I know...I know, I have read these principles over and over in so many books and at first they just seemed to be gibberish. Then I started looking at each word and asked myself how can these elements and principles be applied to a basic block quilt or an art quilt? Look at each item below, they will be found in almost every art book you read.

These are my own interpretations and I make no claim to being an art teacher.

Elements of Art:
Line
Texture
Value
Shape
Color

Line

This can represent diagonal blocks on point or lines of fabric squares that lead your eye around a quilt such as found in an Irish Chain or a Double Wedding Ring. In an art quilt the scene can point with fabric or details in the design, directing your eye to the main focus of a quilt.

The last time I went to an art museum, I paid close attention to the line and directions in those paintings. I found myself looking for the line or the direction the artist wanted me to see. In some cases I had to follow the direction of the people's eyes in the painting that guided me to the main focus the artist wanted me to see.

I viewed a painting where there were a dozen angels all over the canvas and all were looking in the direction of an infant in the bottom right quadrant of the painting. Interestingly, there was one solo angel in the left quadrant that was looking straight ahead off the canvas. I was first lead to the baby and then I looked into the eyes of the angel who was looking in a different direction than all the other angels. What was he looking at? The painter got me with the changes

TRIP AROUND THE WORLD IN 80 DAYS, 90" x 90".
Designed, pieced, and quilted by the author.

in the direction, they brought me in, and made me study the painting.

At first, a quilt depicting a violent storm with dark, ominous clouds in the sky and the trees practically leaning over, sounds too chaotic to find a line. However, the direction of the trees is an easy way to tell which way the wind was blowing and how much tension there is in the air.

In TRIP AROUND THE WORLD IN 80 DAYS, look at the dark line of blocks that goes around the quilt and intercepts the hot air balloon and the mariner's compass. This line is bold and brings your eyes around the quilt to the focus areas of the compass and the hot air balloon. Normally in a square composition the center is the main focus, but I wanted to change things up so I used the strong line to guide the eye to the focus areas.

Texture

An artist sometimes sketches with a pencil and makes solid, heavy shading, or creates texture with little dashes, dots, very faint shading, or what I refer to as fuzzy outlines all to achieve the texture the artist wants in a drawing. In quilting we can create texture with our backfill which can be heavy stippling or lighter texture by doing crosshatching or creating pebbles by doing many different small circles of various sizes as is shown in fig. 2–1.

In my introduction I discussed how a dark color in quilting can be more noticeable because it is surrounded by lighter fabrics. In the TRIP AROUND THE WORLD IN 80 DAYS, there was a strong

brownish-black circle of squares around the center of the quilt. Normally, this feature would have been great, bringing the eye to the center of the quilt, but it was so strong I didn't want the center to be the main focus. I wanted the balloon and compass to be the focus areas. By changing the texture of the quilting around that center of brownish-black line of blocks with what I call fuzzy stippling, it softened the edges. This made the squares recede to open up the quilt and allow the viewer to follow the lines around to the compass and balloon. I was given this idea when I studied a painting of a stream. There were rocks on the surface that looked crystal clear, but the rocks of similar colors, which were underwater, looked so realistic. The artist decided to fuzz the outline and shapes of these rocks, blurring the edges. This texture gave the submerged rocks an almost photo-like appearance.

Fig. 2–1. Close up of TRIP AROUND THE WORLD IN 80 DAYS with fuzzy lines. Full quilt on p. 20.

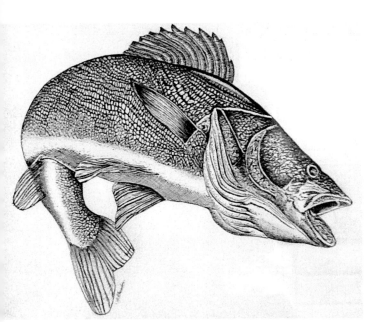

Fig. 2–2. Fish drawing by my daughter, Angela Rhoades.

Fig. 2–3. Closeup of TRIP AROUND THE WORLD IN 80 DAYS showing different values. Full quilt on p. 20.

Value

An artist can achieve value in a pencil sketch by pressing down hard and giving a very dark shading. She can also lighten up on her touch and give a medium value or with the lightest of touches, barely shade with her pencil so that the shading is very faint and light. The values in fig. 2–2 allow for the fish to be depicted in great detail.

In fabric we have many different types of prints, colors, and values. If you want to have value change in a solid fabric it can be done. You can take one color range of fabric, let's say red for my example, and still achieve value changes. You can have some rich burgundy reds representing the darkest value, and a medium red which is close to a pure red, and the lightest being pink.

If you were painting the above values, you would take a pure red and add a touch of black to achieve the dark value. The unenhanced red would be the medium color. To achieve the lightest values of red you would add white and it would become pinkish in color, the lightest value. Experiment with acrylic paint and it will help you understand how to change value.

In fabric, you don't add white because the fabric starts out as white. People who dye fabric can add a touch of black to the red color dye and it forms a dark burgundy color. If they used the red straight it would be the medium value. To achieve the lightest value, dilute the color with more water to produce a washed out pink color. This is the lightest value because the dyer is letting most of the white show through with just a little color. So you can have dark to medium to light value in one color range. You can have as many gradations as you want simply by the amount of water you put in each dye batch.

When doing a Bargello quilt, (a quilt made of strips of fabric sewn together to create movement), you will sometimes be told to do three color runs. No matter what color you choose to use, you will need to pick out the darkest to medium to the lightest. Sometimes they require seven fabrics from darkest value to lightest. With quilting, you can change the value of a color by using a darker or lighter color of thread.

I myself usually like to cut up a piece of fabric that has, for the most part, the color value I want, but has a print of white flowers in it. When it is pieced I see parts of the value I want, but the white flowers are sprinkled around and give such an interesting look to the overall quilt. This is not what you are normally taught, but I love the unexpected twinkle in the quilt (fig. 2–3). When I first started piecing, this was the hardest concept for me to understand. I thought I should only use solid fabrics or fabrics close to solids in color when doing any pattern that relied heavily on value. However, I found the quilts more exciting with a variety of fabrics in the various values, rather than just all solids.

My friend, Mary Sue Suit, pays very little attention to color when she makes a quilt as she considers value the most important aspect. She'll start throwing fabric on the floor and look for the value changes that she wants from dark to medium to light. They could be any color or style of fabric as long as they look good together and have the value changes she wants. She often jokes she doesn't know what a color wheel looks like. Value is everything to her. Personally, I use the color wheel when I get stuck and need a little help, but I know that I need value changes in the colors to make a successful quilt.

Shape

In quilting, shape can be the quilted motif or an appliqué piece. To enhance a shape, maybe it's an appliqué, stipple next to it. This is a positive feature on the quilt. The stippling becomes a negative space and the un-quilted appliqué shape becomes more noticeable. If you chalked in a shape and just stippled around it, you would still be able to make out the shape of the object as if the line was actually quilted or appliquéd in the quilt. The negative quilting creates the positive.

Modern quilts have large spaces of negative quilting, but the positive space, many times a geometric shape, are left un-quilted so that the outline is a relief area.

Color

Color can draw attention like red or be more relaxing and soothing with blues and greens. By choosing the right colors, you can seal the deal when it comes to creating a quilt that represents a certain mood you want to achieve.

Remember, when using the bright warm colors (yellow, red, or orange) you need a much larger percentage of cool or darker colors (purples, blues, dark greens) to balance the strong impact of the warm colors. This might be two to three times the amount of cool colors.

The color and value of the threads you select on a quilt can be subtle and blend into the fabric by using a similar value as the fabric (it doesn't have to be the same color, just blend-able). You can use the same color but just a shade darker or lighter in value than the fabric. The thread you select can also be in-your-face and become part of the major design elements in a quilt, such as using black thread with a white background. I usually strive for the quilting being an equal partner in a quilt and not taking it over, but then not being invisible either. It certainly depends on the quilt and the effect you want to achieve.

Principles:
Unity and Variety
Focal Point
Rhythm
Motion
Balance and symmetry
Space and depth
Scale and proportion

Unity and Variety

Even though you want variety in a quilt to make it interesting you have to create unity so that the quilt, as a whole, looks like it all belongs together. In my example of using spirals for the quilting (p. 14), if I hadn't mixed up the shapes and sizes of the spirals it would be plain and boring.

In my photo there are all the different types of fruit, but it's unified because it's all the same subject matter. Notice they are all different sizes, shapes, and colors, but they have unity as the theme (fig. 2–4).

Many of the traditional quilters of the past just used crosshatching. It was done beautifully, but if you compare the quilts of old to the quilts of today, the variety of line work is stimulating. You could have curved crosshatching, straight line borders, inside the crosshatching every other line is stippled, or the line can be wavy. All the various different types of lines bring unity to the quilt because the lines are repeated in different ways throughout the quilt.

See what I have done with crosshatching in BLACK TIE GALA (fig. 2–5) and curvy crosshatching in TUSCANY MEMORIES (fig. 2–6).

I repeated the spirals in the embroidery into the quilting design in the middle of FAIRY DUST (fig. 2–7, p. 26) and EMERGING SPRING (fig. 2–8, p. 26).

Fig. 2–4.

Fig. 2–5. BLACK TIE GALA, detail. Full quilt on p. 35.

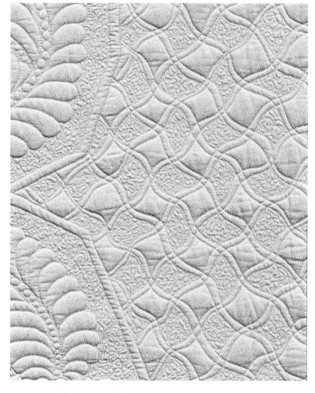

Fig. 2–6. TUSCANY MEMORIES, curvy crosshatching detail. Full quilt on p. 28.

Fig. 2–7. Variety of backfill, **FAIRY DUST**, detail. Full quilt on p. 18.

Fig. 2–8. **EMERGING SPRING,** close up detail of spirals. Full quilt on p. 11.

Focal Point

There are so many different ideas from different painters and quilters about where a person should put the main focal point in their art. I found it all so confusing. There was even some Greek formula that with my lacking algebra skills was not for me. Finally, I came across several artists, I can't remember their names, but they gave me the best help I could use in an art quilt, fig. 2–9.

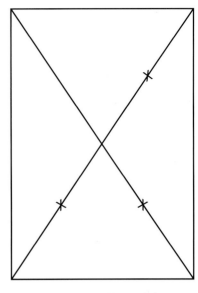

The instructions were to divide the quilt or canvas diagonally from corner to corner. Approximately halfway between the center and the corner in the left bottom quadrant, the right bottom quadrant, or the right top quadrant were excellent places for a focal point. I found most artists said they never put a focal point in the top left quadrant.

Fig. 2–9. Drawing where to focus

Not believing everything I read, I decided to do an experiment on TRIP AROUND THE WORLD IN 80 DAYS. In the top left corner I put the wind blowing using shiny metallic thread and hundreds of crystals. I quilted the wind blowing over to the hot air balloon and down to the Mariner's compass (fig. 2–10). At the quilt show, I turned my name tag around and stood where I could watch the people's eyes as they looked at the quilt and maybe only 20% of the people even looked up into that corner. I wasted a lot of thread and crystals where no one bothered to look. I became a believer that maybe these artists knew what they were talking about. Bear in mind if you are doing a square composition, most of the time the focus or focal point is somewhere near the center of the quilt.

Note: In Strengthening the Design, pp. 40–43, you will see how I use backfill to help show off the focal points and add variety to a quilt.

Fig. 2–10. TRIP AROUND THE WORLD IN 80 DAYS, detail, left focus spot. Full quilt on p. 20.

TUSCANY MEMORIES, *77" x 77"*. Designed and quilted by the author.

THE ART OF Quilting ♡ Judy Woodworth

Rhythm

The repetition of designs in a quilt can be accented with backfill and it will create harmony in the entire quilt. That is why, though I may use many different types of backfill, I try to repeat them throughout the quilt so that it creates the harmony I am looking for (fig. 2–11).

Motion

This can be the illusion of movement. It can be blurred, quiet, or implied. Remember when I told you about the quilt where the trees were bent over and you could tell there was wind, although it was only implied. Also, the movement of the water was shown by the blurred objects under the water, these are prime examples of the illusion of movement.

In quilting, we can create lots of motion with curvy lines, and circles. In backfill, I love creating movement with curvy crosshatching with circles and straight crosshatching inside the circles for a bit of variety as in Easy Diamonds (fig. 2–12, p. 31). It creates movement and a rhythm in a quilt.

Avatar Revisited is an award winning quilt. It won Best Longarm Quilt at QuiltWeek®– Paducah, Kentucky, 2012. This close up really shows movement in a quilt (fig. 2–13, p. 31).

RIGHT: **Fig. 2–11. Tuscany Memories,** detail. Full quilt on p. 28.

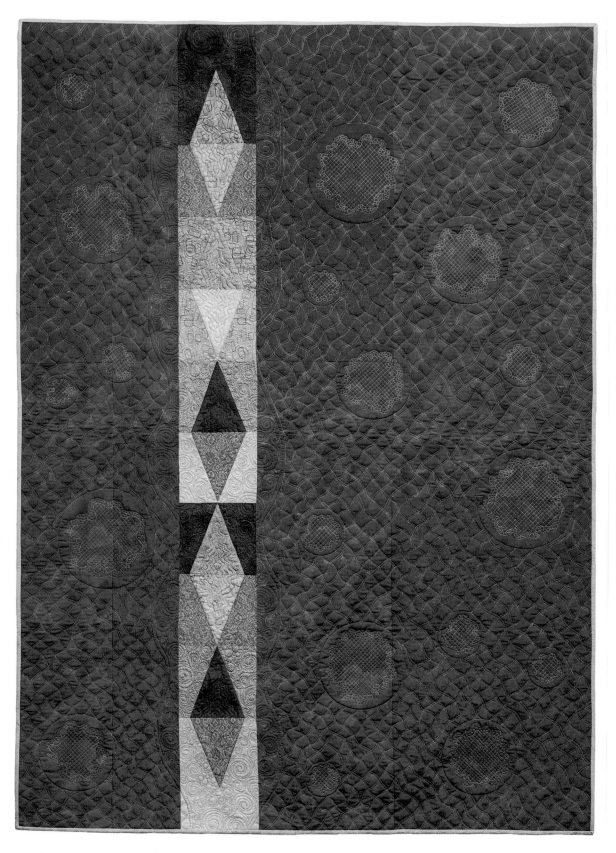

EASY DIAMONDS, 49" x 66". Pieced by Mary Sue Suit, Sidney, Nebraska. Quilted by the author.

Balance and Symmetry

An example of distribution of weight is easily found in nature. This one is especially wonderful in a quilt. I have noticed more quilt judges like things balanced and symmetrical. Not to say asymmetrical quilts are not accepted, but even they need to be well balanced.

This detail picture of EMERGING SPRING was taken just after quilting and still shows the blue water soluble marker (fig. 2–14, p. 32). If you notice I sectioned off where the feather would be and then quilted it freemotion.

There are areas of heavier quilting and some lighter areas of quilting, but because they are distributed equally throughout the quilt they appear to be well balanced. The overall quilt is symmetrical and I tried to make the quilting symmetrical also.

Space and Depth

You can create space and depth with the correct placement of the values. You can make a three dimensional quilt or create a different perspective.

I was able to create depth in the hot air balloon by carefully choosing lighter fabrics where the sun was shining down on the balloon. I used darker colors and the curved pieces to make your eye see the hot air balloon so that it had depth and wasn't flat (fig. 2–15, p. 32).

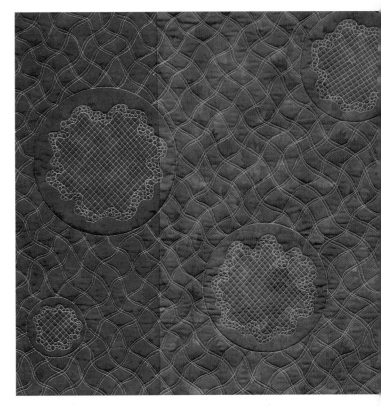

Fig. 2–12. EASY DIAMONDS, detail. Full quilt on p. 30.

Fig. 2–13. AVATAR REVISTED, detail. Full quilt on p. 67 of *Make Your Own Quilting Designs & Patterns* by the author.

Fig. 2–14. EMERGING SPRING, detail still shows blue soluble marker. Full quilt on p. 11.

Fig. 2–15. TRIP AROUND THE WORLD IN 80 DAYS, detail. Full quilt on p. 20.

Space in quilting is usually achieved when you have more intense quilting and leave other areas not quilted as heavily. Another way to show space is by having a large amount of background fabric in your piecing. The space (or plain background fabric) actually helps bring your eye to the main focus of a quilt and is usually achieved by leaving an area un-quilted, such as in an appliqué. A heavily quilted area, with stippling or crosshatching, is a space for your eye to rest. In whole cloth quilts, I always have to remind my students that they need to include more white space so that the designs are not too close together or they could lose the main focal points in the design.

Scale and Proportion

The scale and size needs to be in the correct proportion as in nature. For example, in an art quilt, a bird needs to be larger than a butterfly. The butterfly would need to be in the correct proportion to the bird to be believable as a real life interpretation. Of course, there are crazy art quilts where all the sizes are mixed up, but we are talking about a realistic picture.

When I designed the quilt BUTTERFLY FANTASY, I was trying to make the lilies fit in the right proportion inside the enclosed appliqué sections. Not too big and not too small. One of the judges said the butterfly was not in the correct proportion to the flowers. I was trying to get the butterflies to scale to fit nicely in the enclosed half square area, but I certainly understood where the judge was coming from.

FANTASY BUTTERFLY, 68" x 68". Designed, pieced, appliquéd, and quilted by the author.

ART TECHNIQUES IN QUILTING

Using all those art theories and putting them into practice in a quilt is my very favorite thing to do. Just a reminder, all things in art are subject to your own interpretation. If fifty quilters decided to do the same quilt you will probably get fifty different versions. Some may be stronger than others, but there is not a right or wrong way. I can't stress enough, you are the artist. Follow your instincts and you will be fine.

Now I ask myself, how can I show you about art in a way that will let you understand my process? How do I try to incorporate these art principles and elements into my designing and quilting? The best way to do this is to take you through my quiting process. I'll discuss my own interpretation of art and how I assimilated these principles into my final decisions. It's usually the number one question my students ask me, "How do you decide what to quilt?" So let's begin.

I have been making so many symmetrical quilts lately I decided to make an asymmetrical quilt, one that would have viewers engage the border.

When I first drew the design, I decided I was going to use black fabric for the long spikes and knew they would look like black ties. From this decision it was a no brainer that I would name it BLACK TIE GALA. I picked the rest of the colors that would create a festive and dramatic event with golden flames. I knew the background color should be an exciting and dramatic red to help create the romantic mood (fig. 3–1). There also had to be black and white piano keys. Once the colors were selected and it was pieced and appliquéd, I used music as the theme of my quilting to go with the mood of the quilt.

Fig. 3–1. Choosing fabric

BLACK TIE GALA, *67" x 71". Designed, pieced, appliquéd, and quilted by the author.*

Fig. 3–2. Designing process

Fig. 3–3. Patterns

Fig. 3–4. Piano keys pieced

Whenever I design my quilts, I am always thinking about giving myself large areas to quilt. I love to quilt so this is important to me. A person who loves to piece might have had the mariner's compass take up the entire area, planning only to do ditch work, and to show off her piecing. That's the fun thing about designing your own quilt, it can fit your personal preferences in your design (figs. 3–2 and 3–3).

I was on a star quilter's panel once at a big quilt show. The only judge on the panel was explaining how quilts needed to have harmony and she was describing a quilt that had a red, white, and blue giraffe. She said the colors didn't match with the mood of the rest of the quilt. Immediately, I started thinking to myself: if I put the giraffe in a parade with other animals in the same color scheme, it would make for a whimsical, patriotic quilt. The quilting could be fireworks going off in the background to further develop the theme.

Never say never, there is always a way to incorporate your design ideas.

In Black Tie Gala, the quilt is very contemporary and the whimsical design went with the mood of the quilt (fig. 3–4). The colors selected for the quilt and the quilting matched the theme of the quilt. In fact, this quilt won second place in the musical theme category of a major quilt show. In the outside border, I quilted the sound system with sound waves. In Freemotion Quilting Combinations, pp. 60–62, you will see how I quilted those ribbons of sound.

This is the back of BLACK TIE GALA and it is showing off the different colors of thread and the musical theme (fig. 3–5).

As you can see, BLACK TIE GALA is heavily quilted because it is a wall quilt and a show quilt. Throughout the entire quilt I used a variety of backfill for interest and excitement with the music theme being the dominate quilting design. It was important to create rhythm in this quilt to give it movement and excitement.

Sometimes you can quilt in extra star points to give the star a more interesting look and create some positive and negative quilting (fig. 3–6).

Note: In Freemotion Quilting Combinations, p. 58, you will see I have quilted the black tie points and how I surrounded the smaller spikes with two lines and an interesting stippled surround. I have used straight crosshatching in the middle of the quilt, but used curvy lines of the sheet music and notes in the next area to create a variation of the lines. I quilted around the notes three or more times so they would really stand out. This also helped me quilt the design non-stop as I quilted the double curvy lines of the music and around each note.

Deciding what to quilt is all about creating harmony between the quilt top and the quilting design. In most cases, the quilting should be an equal partner in the final product. Occasionally, when a quilt is very busy, the quilting should be more subtle so that the quilt doesn't have too many distracting points. Other times the quilt

Fig. 3–5. Back detail of **BLACK TIE GALA.** Full quilt on p. 35

Fig. 3–6. Creating new star points

top is very simple and it needs some colorful quilting and interesting negative and positive quilting to kick the quilt up to the next level. The modern quilts we see today are simple with the geometric quilted shapes that create interesting texture, open spaces, and contrast.

Just to finish, if you are one of those people who pick out your colors of fabric based on a theme, be careful. You need to use the same percentage of colors in your focus fabric in a matching fabric value for the rest of your quilt. That is only if you want to keep the same mood and effect as the focus fabric.

Fig. 3–7. An example of focus fabric.

This is a focus fabric I used early in my quilting career (fig. 3–7). As you can see, I used a large amount of the pink and the dark green in my pieced top. When I was done, I was so unhappy because it didn't capture the mood that was in the focus fabric. The colors I chose were pretty close, but it just didn't have that subtle, almost ethereal, feeling. It took me a while to figure it out, but I should have used approximately the same amount of dark, medium, and light values as in the focus fabric to achieve the same soothing look of the focus fabric (fig. 3–8).

Fig. 3–8. Focus fabric used incorrectly.

If you look at the focus fabric, about 80% of the fabric is very light value with subtle greens and beiges. There is only a little bit of darker pink and only a tiny amount of dark green. If I had used mostly the light values in about 80% of the quilt top, the quilt would have been more peaceful. To capture the mood of tranquility I should have been willing to have more of a blended lighter valued quilt with less contrast. Yes, usually when picking fabric and thread it is important to have a good variety of light, medium, and dark. However, there are some quilts where, to keep them calm and serene, there should be a few value changes.

The choice of thread colors you use can make or break a quilt depending on what effect and mood you are depicting.

If I'm doing a traditional quilt I try very hard to choose the same or just slightly darker shade of thread as the fabric. My quilting needs to be very subtle and not take over the traditional top. It doesn't mean I can't quilt it heavily, it just means I want to blend with the fabric. *Example:* quilting white fabric with white thread. However, if I'm doing a quilt like BLACK TIE GALA, I can use lots of fun and exciting colors to match the mood of the quilt.

RIGHT: **Fig. 3–9. BLACK TIE GALA**, detail of quilting. Full quilt on p. 35.

STRENGTHENING THE DESIGN

ROSES BETWEEN FRIENDS, 92" x 100". Designed and pieced by the Mary Sue Suit, Sidney, Nebraska. Quilted by the author.

When I first saw Mary Sue Suit's pieced quilt, ROSES BETWEEN FRIENDS, I put it up on my design board and studied it. Although this wasn't a true traditional quilt design it had the mood of a traditional, elegant quilt. The roses were beautiful and truly the focus of the quilt. I personally thought that the quilting should really show off the roses. Mary Sue's intention was for this quilt to be on a bed, and she doesn't mind it being heavily quilted. Some people like lighter or medium quilting for a bed quilt. So the second thing I did was put the un-quilted pieced top on a bed and studied it some more. I also turned it several times to decide how the center would best look. Eventually, I determined the rectangle center looked best vertically.

Usually I am elated when I have this much white space to

quilt, but I decided that I needed to do the traditional crosshatching in some of the white so that the roses would be the show stopper that they are. I usually start my design in the middle and work out a layer at a time. It's intimidating at first because all you see is a big empty canvas. I've found that by starting on one area and completing the design I can move to the next border and make design decisions for the rest of the quilting. Some quilters like to design from the outside in. It just works for them. For me, I have to start in the middle.

The minute I saw the center of this quilt, it just cried out to me to have initials in it like older quilts. I printed several different sizes of initials and laid them directly on the fabric to give me an idea of size and scale, fig. 4–1. I knew to show off the initials and make them faux trapunto, I would have to use two battings on the entire quilt. Usually for show quilts I use thicker wool batting for the top and an 80/20 batting next to the backing. In this quilt I used the 80/20 and a bamboo batting on top because I knew Mary Sue likes the bamboo batting. In using this batting I knew I would need to do a micro stippling next to the initials to have them pop up.

I transferred the initials to the quilt by putting the printed initials under the quilt top and using a light box, marked the top with a blue water soluble marker. I used the water soluble marker because I knew Mary Sue had prewashed her fabric to avoid bleeding so when we washed and rinsed the finished quilted top in cold water to block it, we know it wouldn't bleed. I decided to enclose the initials in an oval as the middle section is a rectangle and not a square (fig 4–2). This way I could do the double crosshatching on the outside areas of the oval (fig 4–3, p. 42). I used both stippling next to the initials and small circles (or pebbles) to the oval edge.

To design the next area, I laid freezer paper over the quilt top above the next border and traced the outline of the border with a blue water soluble marker. I didn't want to trace with pencil or black sharpie in case I pushed too hard, broke through the freezer paper, and accidentally drew on the quilt top. After this, I moved the blue marked freezer paper away from the quilt top to start

Fig. 4–1.

Fig. 4–2.

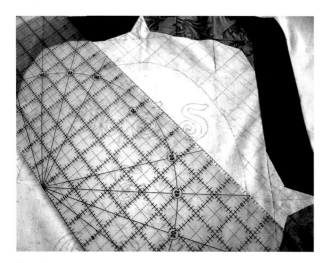

Fig. 4–3.

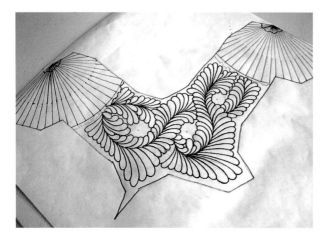

Fig. 4–4.

Fig. 4–5.

designing. I drew the feathers with a pencil, erasing and improving the design as I went along. Once it was perfected and just the way I wanted it, I retraced the feathers with a black Sharpie® marker so that when I put the design under the quilt top and used a light box I would be able to easily see the design.

This is a symmetrical quilt, using the mirror image, all I had to do was trace one section. For the next section, I turned the freezer paper over for the mirror image design and traced it to the top (fig. 4–4). You can see through the freezer paper from both sides, so the design is easily mirrored which saves you from having to redraw the design again in mirror (or reverse) image.

To make sure I liked the initials and could see them, I sprayed the center with Blue Line Eraser™ so I could see what it looked like without the blue water soluble markings (fig. 4–5). It would be completely rinsed off after being quilted, but I wanted to see what it would look like without the blue markings.

I needed to connect the quilting between the two pink roses so the next area where I planned to do the double crosshatching would have a new stop point. By crosshatching in the next section it would tie in with the same crosshatching from the middle of the quilt. Repetition is very important. Carrying the design to another area of the quilt keeps harmony in the quilting.

To do this I used small circles inside a pointed outlined section that looked good with the curved lines in the piecing. Otherwise, I would have had to do the crosshatching all the way to the radiating lines around the points of the ribbon pieced section. I needed circles to break from the two types of lines and create a division between the radiating lines as well as the crosshatching. Since there are circles in the middle it is important that I use circles somewhere else in the quilt and this was a perfect little pocket to put more (fig. 4–6).

Fig. 4–6.

When I teach whole cloth quilting, the hardest concept for beginners is that sometimes you just need a white space, a calm place for your eyes to rest, and the double crosshatching gives you that perfect spot for calm in the quilt (fig. 4–7). It would be easy to want to fill that second border with more feathers or design, but sometimes simple quilting is what you need for that white space.

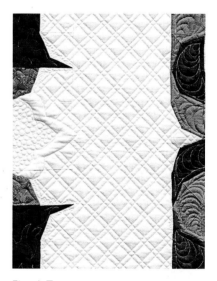

Fig. 4–7.

After I quilted the texture in the ribbon, I wanted feathers next to the outside border for repetition. In the feathered border I did freemotion feathers about the same size as the feathers surrounding the middle. I had the feathers changing directions all around that outside border. Not exactly a mirror image symmetrical border design, but it also wasn't going in a one direction design. By putting in more radiating lines in a half circle around the outside points I was able to quilt in the areas next to the roses with freemotion feathers (fig. 4–8).

The completed quilt looks really nice on a bed with lots of repetition in the design, harmony in the quilting, and a variety of radiating lines and crosshatching for the background. It's interesting, but somewhat traditional looking, to match the mood of the quilt. I also used one color of thread, white cotton Auriful™ 60-weight, so that the thread matched the feel of a traditional quilt and blended in evenly with the colored areas of the roses. With all the ditch work that was required and backtracking, it was important that I used a very fine thread to make the backtracking almost invisible. See ROSES BETWEEN FRIENDS, on p. 40.

Fig. 4–8.

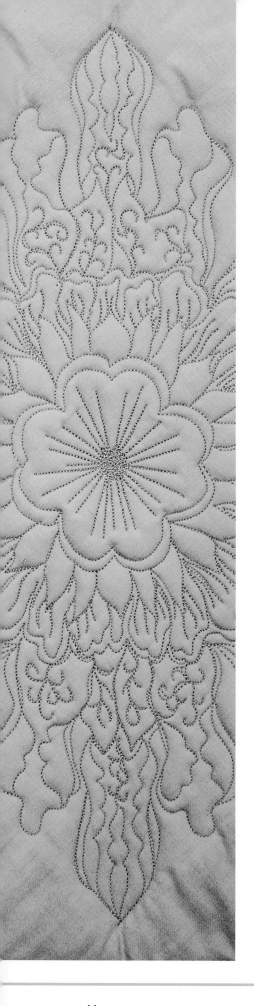

PERSPECTIVES ON APPLICATION

Below, I have shared various pieces of advice for the longarm machine, the home sewing machine, and various ideas on products to use, and how to improve your quilting. Enjoy.

Physical Environment

↩ At any time if you drop a pin on the floor, stop immediately and pick it up.

↩ Use a magnet (the kind that holds broaches for pins) to hold your scissors, or put a magnet in safe place on your longarm quilting machine, away from the computer, for your scissors.

↩ Think about the sounds in your room: soft slow music, hard-rock, background white noise like the news, no noise, or maybe audible books? What helps you create?

↩ Decide how much organization your quilting room requires for you to continue working through all your projects and quilting. You need to be able to be in your Zen creative space. If you must have "things always in a perfect organizational order" for you to quilt or design, do it. Otherwise relax just a little, as long as you know where things are.

↩ Keep body and hands in an ergonomic position when you quilt or use rulers.

↩ Learn to quilt with a chair if you are using a longarm. A 30½" tall engineer's saddle seat is what I use.

LEFT: Pattern 21 quilted sample detail, see pattern on p. 89.

Use plastic containers for storage for gadgets, or hang them on a work board with clips, or use a kitchen dish pan drainer for storage.

Sam's Club® has very inexpensive plastic banquet tables that you can set up in your garage or outside if there is no room in your house to block.

Wash hands before you touch a quilt.

Put on a clean apron (or fleece jacket each day, especially if you have dogs).

Always keep your quilting room, machine, and floors clean.

Try to keep the table, the pantograms side, clean with no papers, or sticky pads, or junk. (This one is hard for me.)

Every day, clean this table with a damp cloth to make sure no oil drops.

If you find threads on your carpeted floor, use a new, clean toilet brush to grab them up.

Room set up is the most important. Put your sewing machine in a corner. An "L" shaped table is best, but you can use two tables placed as a L. This way the quilt will not fall off the table as walls will gently gather the quilt that is not being quilted.

If you do get oil on your quilts, after you cry for a minute, dab it with Sew Clean.

After I advance the quilt, I use shipping tape to remove any loose threads, or pet hairs.

Preparation

Set yearly goals. This year I will learn how to do ditch quilting. Or use gadgets, or learn a new feather.

Keep sketch books of your drawings or doodles. I don't take the time to put a printed picture in a scrap book for each customer's quilts. I tried this but it takes too long to print out and put in a scrapbook. Time is money for me.

Stop if you have been quilting a little while and drink water. Get up and walk around.

After every two hours take a 15 minute break.

Roll your shoulders. Shake your head "yes" and "no" to relieve tension.

Lie down and elevate your legs, close your eyes and look for inspiration on how to quilt next.

Wear the best shoes you can afford.

Remember to take lots of breaks, and roll your shoulders so that your back doesn't get all tight. If you quilt too long, you are just going to have to start ripping. So relax, enjoy, and take breaks at least every two hours.

Your arms should be bent perpendicular to the sewing area in a comfortable position, thus the table and sewing machine have to be at the proper height. If you have to put your sewing chair and peddle on a higher platform, do this if you are really short.

People who learn how to hand quilt say it takes them about one large quilt to learn how to get in a rhythm and do the running stitch.

Home sewing machine people tell me it usually takes practicing on several baby quilts or utility quilts to get the speed and hand movement coordinated. So just don't give up.

Start with the no stress quilts, and then when you are confident you can do some of your show or heirloom quilts.

Tools

I recommend using side clamps on a longarm. Not tight or taut just even and straight.

My suggestion for clipping threads scissors, Gingher®. It looks like a bird.

Also use a small magnet to hold needles to tie knots in quilts to bury thread tails.

In your apron, keep the gadgets you are using for the day so they are in easy reach.

Also keep marking tools in your apron.

Marking tools I most use: Avery or Bohin chalk pens, blue water soluble, and Blue Line Erasers. Chalk mechanical pencils by Bohin, Fons and Porter, or SewLine.

Circle Gadgets work great for cross-hatching. Get circles all sizes with quartering lines but also side line divisions. Just follow the line as you advance with the circles.

Keep a protractor handy for equal divisions of radiating lines.

Blue Line Eraser™ product does not erase purple air erasing pens. Spray the purple air markings if they don't disappear by themselves with water. www.bluelineeraser.com

Purple air disappearing pens take a day or two in my dry area to disappear but in moist areas of the country the marks can disappear in an hour or so.

Be careful to not use yellow marking tools. They don't work for me. Use caution.

Synthrapol® gently dabbed on does remove some yellow marks, or Sew Clean.

If using the blue chalk powder, get the kind that can be removed with heat. Pam Clark recommends Sew Clean for removing blue chalk powder marks.

Best needles for tying off thread: embroidery needles or needles with a slit.

Ripping out quilting is not fun. I use the tip of my Gingher scissors, or a seam ripper every fourth stitch. Advance until you see the back and you can just grab the loose thread and pull it out.

You can use a circle template guide, found in an engineer's section of an office supply store, to mark circles. After you have been quilting for a while you won't need to mark.

Use lighting tracks above your longarm, but turn them off when quilting white fabric with white thread.

℮⊃ Always have a place for your 120" measuring tool. Mine is draped on the edge of my quilting frame.

℮⊃ Keep an assortment of big square rulers, and 24" rulers, and L shaped sheet-rock tools, and other items to keep straight lines even.

℮⊃ Tape on a silicon sheet so the quilt glides easy. Leave a hole for the needle area for your home sewing machine.

℮⊃ Use quilting gloves that have little grips.

℮⊃ When you are first learning, mark your design with chalk or use water soluble pen (provided you can wash the quilt in cold clear water and the fabric won't bleed). It's easier to follow a design at first. Later you can learn freemotion. Even with freemotion you might want to mark just a few lines.

Machine

℮⊃ Oil and maintain your machine.

℮⊃ Check tension every time you change the bobbin, oil, and clean out lint.

℮⊃ Fudge the tension by tightening the top more, just a little, because you can't keep an eye on the back as you quilt, and bad tension always shows up on the back of a quilt.

℮⊃ Use a magnification glass to check tension on the top and bottom before you begin quilting.

℮⊃ Use scraps of similar fabric on the side next to the quilt to test tension.

℮⊃ You need balanced tension.

Thread

℮⊃ The higher number the thread, such as 60 or 100-weight,

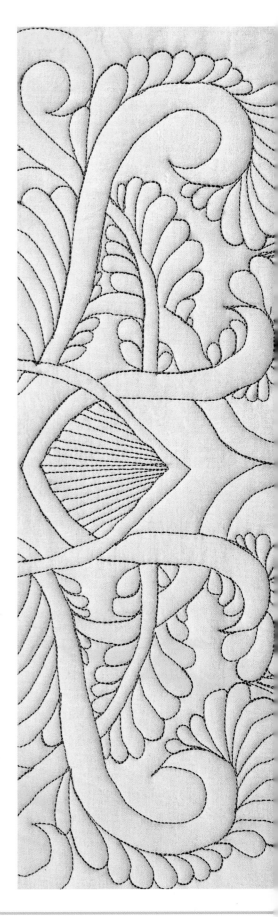

RIGHT: Pattern 12 quilted sample detail, see pattern on p. 80.

will be really light thread and good for backtracking or ditch work, or heavy backfill.

℮ᴗ The lower the number of thread, such as 35-weight, will be that in-your-face-thread.

℮ᴗ For most general quilting use 40 or 50-weight thread.

℮ᴗ Use silk thread with caution. Silk fabric and thread may not survive as many years as cotton, so use these threads and fabrics at your risk.

℮ᴗ Decide how you want to store thread not used. For me, it works to put them by brand and color in plastic bins. It keeps them clean of dust and not too big of a problem with loose winding threads unless it's metallic. You may want to put a net over those slippery thread cones.

℮ᴗ To keep thread from getting stuck in the split and breaking at the bottom of the spool, use net or a foam cushion pad to set these threads on.

℮ᴗ Use the same type of thread in the top and in the bobbin, with some exceptions. Use Fil-Tec™ Glide pre-wound bobbins (www.fil-tec.com) natural with white, beige or gold thread on the top, or with other lighter colors and it blends in beautiful.

℮ᴗ I also like Superior® bottom line thread. www.superiorthreads.com

℮ᴗ YLI recommends using a soft touch thread with metallic thread on top. www.ylicorp.com

℮ᴗ Many different award winning quilters really love using metallic threads. They recommend Yenmet, and YLI metallic thread. www.redrockthreads.com

℮ᴗ I also like YLI silk metallic thread.

LEFT: Pattern 7 quilted sample detail, see pattern on p. 75.

Make your own decisions about linty thread. I hate it and won't use it.

Set your machine up with a thread dispenser close so you can change thread without having to walk to the back and forth to your machine.

Replace guides that thread can slip out of with ceramic fishing guides and cement glue.

Backing/Batting

Load your quilt top, bottom, and backing per your manual instructions for your longarm.

When you pin on the backing on your longarm canvas, roll it all the way to the end (like the quilt is finished) and iron that section right on your machine, pick off any lint. Keep advancing back to the beginning and ironing until it is straight.

If your backing fabric is very soft, I would recommend ironing it with a dry iron and starch before you load it in your machine frame.

If you want Batik as a backing remember to wash it several times so your needle can pierce smoothly through the fabric and not have to blast through the heavily dyed fabric.

Cotton Sateen is a great backing and I do not recommend washing it. If you wash Sateen, it gets too soft and is easy to get tucks on the back.

Check to see if batting needs washing by reading the label. I have not found any that require washing. Even if I am going to block, I only use cold clear water and shrinkage is minimal on most battings. Sometimes it shrinks 1" more going in one direction. Don't sweat this. It's more important it is blocked and lays square.

Show quilts use two battings and usually consist of 80/20 and wool.

A pieced backing that has different types of fabric, some tight weave, some soft, might have a few places with a few tucks because of the different fabrics.

If I have a large backing, I like to pin the selvage on the rollers. This way I know I am starting with very straight backing.

A backing that has stripes or fabric that is pieced in stripes is near impossible to keep the ditch border side lines perfectly parallel to the stripes on the back. Just fore warn them or don't do straight line vertical ditch work that will be different then the stripes on the back.

Double spray starch your fabric for binding before you cut it. It's like cutting perfect paper.

If you have a fabric that has a shiny side, on the dull side take a chalk pencil and mark several lines through the dull side. This is so you can make sure your grain and the shine is on the good side when you make your binding.

Don't be afraid to use wool batting, it quilts like butter and is wonderful for show quilts.

Finishing

When you are all done, if it is your quilt and you know you washed your fabrics, block the quilt by rinsing it in cold water. If not washed you can steam block.

Get it appraised before you send it to a show and get a rider on your homeowner's policy to insure it.

Binding should be sewn with an almost invisible stitch. I have found that the blind stitch (or ladder stitch) works best for me.

Fold the quilt from the top down, almost rolling it the size of the box you will send quilt in, and accordion pleat it to also fit the size of the box lengthwise. I like to ship with Fed-Ex best, but that is only my preference.

Make sure your quilt is clean of any spots, dog hair, or loose threads.

Binding shouldn't be rippled, so block the quilt first and put on binding when it's dry, cut and square.

You get lots of extra points and judge approval if you do unique binding techniques such as piping. If you do a poor job, you don't get difficulty points like in Olympic diving. They love scallops that are well done.

Close the front and back of binding miters with stitches.

Developing the Quilt

Use good art design principles when designing the quilts.

Quilt top and quilting stitching should be well balanced, and integral to the design.

The quilt design should speak to the judge, and be a "wow" first impression.

Piecing must be precise with corners and points matched up. Use Roxanne's Glue Baste-it to match points instead of pens. This really works.

Select the approximate thread and design for the quilt's personality.

Technique

Left handed quilters using gadgets and guides, you are so lucky. Use your left hand to hold and control. Then move the gadgets and guides. Don't use your left hand to start the on and off switch.

Right handers, you will learn to be as good with your left hand as your right hand with practice.

If stalled, take a breath and just start by quilting the border. Once you start quilting you will relax.

Learn several different ways to do circles. Circles that are like a figure eight, or individual circles that advance by moving through an already sewn line. Visualize the center of the circle before you sew it.

I love stitch regulated sewing machines but if you have an older model you will learn when to speed up and when to go at a steady pace through practice so you have even stitches.

Home sewing machines take more practice than the longarm, but I think you can do some incredible small and accurate designs that sometimes the longarmer's can't do. So don't give up and practice, practice, practice.

Quilting

Use your digital camera or cell phone to photograph as you progress.

While you are quilting, if you hear something that sounds different stop and check the bottom and all your thread guides. You might be running out of bobbin thread.

If sewing in manual mode, take off quickly, move evenly, listen to your machine, and be careful on round quilting such as the top of a feather not to move too fast. Strive for consistent even stitches.

At the beginning of a stitch, with stitch regulator, just slightly jiggle to start stitch and start slow, so there is no long stitch at the beginning.

Before you load the top, make a few decisions on what is to be the most important focus in the quilt. Decide a few quilting ideas, but leave some design decisions to serendipity.

Hide your stops and starts in a feather middle seam. Don't start in the middle of a feather. It's better to remove the stitches to a good backtracking spot.

Learn how to do all types of feathers. Bump back feathers invented by Karen McTavish are my very favorite. Learn this first as a beginner. The longer you have been quilting the longarm feathers the longer it takes to learn the bump-back feathers.

Rippled borders can be eased in. Don't use long feathers or designs that will be hard to ease in the extra fullness.

Know where to start sewing in a block when working in the

Pattern 1 quilted sample detail, see pattern on p. 69.

ditch. Never start at the corner. Start 1" from any corner. If you start in a corner ditch, you will probably quilt in a pleat when you quilt back around to the starting point.

Sew around the outside of the quilt edge in ¹⁄₁₆" inside of where binding will go. This stabilizes it before you start quilting.

Do borders next, right side down to within 1" of where you will sew the ditch work across the bottom line. Quilt down the left ditch and across the bottom border, end by sewing up the 1" to connect your borders. This will keep you from getting a pleat.

If you missed the ditch line continue to the end. Go back and correct when you finish.

On all quilts, if I am doing ditch work down the side borders, I always tie my thread because you can see the stops and starts here with the tiny or overlapping stitches. It just shows up more on the ditch.

Leave the two threads as you advance so you can see where to start the next line.

Tie the four threads together and bury.

With thread tails, except in borders or ditch work, I bury or cut these thread tails immediately. Loose thread bothers my creativity. I keep looking at the thread.

Use longarm zippers. I just pin to the zippers but then I am able to take them off and check the design. If you see threads showing through to the front fabric that accidentally got quilted into the batting, safety pin it for later correction. Or use the smallest embroidery hock to pull it out immediately.

Press with a steam iron to take out the pleat you might have just quilted in, right on the roller. There is a memory of where the pleat was and you need to remove it before you re-quilt.

LEFT: Pattern 13 quilted sample detail, see pattern on p. 81.

☞ Keep adding machine tape handy to mark even divisions. Pre-mark with safety pins on the edges of quilts with even divisions if doing overalls. That way the bottom row won't be squished.

☞ I recommend using side clamps. Not tight or taut just even and straight.

☞ When you use advance rollers the top and bottom must be even and straight and definitely not too tight, but not too loose either. Back down one click if not certain.

☞ Tape on a silicon sheet so the quilt glides easy. Leave a hole for the needle area.

☞ Don't roll the quilt when you are machine quilting on your sewing machine. Loosely gather it in your lap and on your table. Concentrate on quilting just the area by the needle. Then stop, with needle down, and move to the next area before you start quilting.

☞ Sometimes you might quilt with the feed dogs up for lines, but the majority of the time you will have your feed dogs lowered so the fabric can move any direction you can.

☞ Don't be afraid to move the quilt through the machine as you count to keep even stitches.

☞ Use a tighter stitch with piecing when using a longarm. When they are loaded with the batting, it tends to pull the thread apart and shows the color of the thread.

☞ Use a light, dark, or neutral color thread for piecing, depending on the fabric.

☞ Curve piecing and appliqué should have smooth round edges.

☞ Points on appliqué should be sharp.

☞ Watch to make sure you have no shadowing either with piecing or appliqué.

☞ If you sew on beads, make sure they are securely applied and knotted more often. Be sure to do this after quilting and stay in the batting to pass to the next area.

☞ If you do trapunto don't let the trapunto batting "seep" out of edges of quilting line.

☞ Quilting needs to have even, consistent stitches. Big one for judges.

☞ Quilting should be evenly distributed.

☞ Make sure to have invisible starts and stops for quilting.

☞ Don't forget to quilt a little in the appliqué if big, or in the embroidery. You don't want baggy appliqué areas.

☞ Don't run up over the edge when doing in-the-ditch around applique.

☞ Borders should be straight, and corners should be square. Check with rulers.

FREEMOTION QUILTING COMBINATIONS

SAMPLE, 25" x 35". Made by the author. Painted by Bill Woodworth, Rapid City, South Dakota.

The orange border from the sample was roughly drawn from a Dover® book design. The balance of the design was original (fig. 6–1b).

For the line and circles freemotion crosshatching design (figs. 6–1 and 6-1b), pre-chalk a few uneven divisions and then chalk which direction of lines and where to put the circles. I usually try to make the horizontal divisions fairly even by using adding machine tape and folding it to the size I want the horizontal lines at. The vertical lines are uneven and not matching.

Variations of mixing backfill are featured in figs. 6–2 and 6–3.

Odd shapes with interesting radiating lines filled with ribbon candy designs make this freemotion design really interesting. It creates movement, with positive and negative space (fig. 6–3).

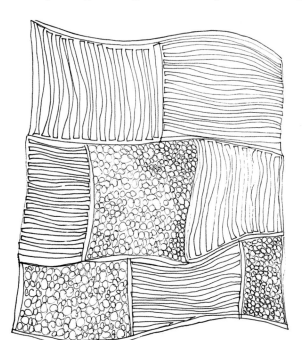

Fig. 6–1. Freemotion 1

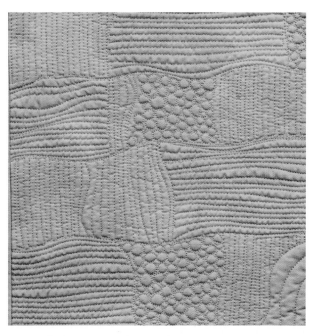

Fig. 6–1b. Freemotion 1, sample

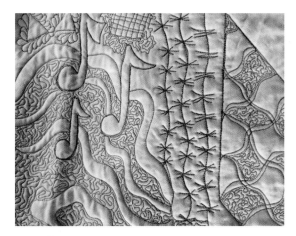

Fig. 6–2. Freemotion variation

Fig. 6–3. Freemotion variation

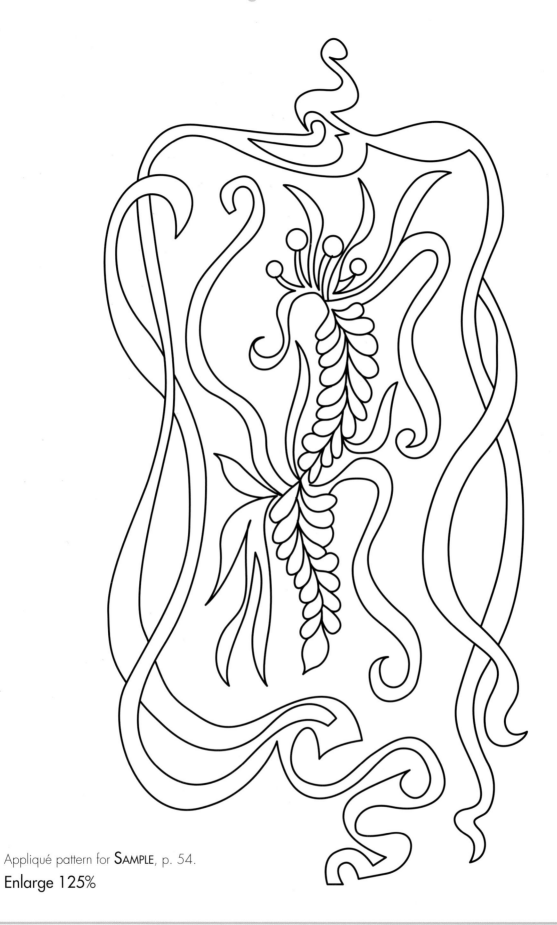

Appliqué pattern for SAMPLE, p. 54.

Enlarge 125%

I love this woven design. Follow it step by step in figs. 6–5a through 6–5i.

Fig. 6–5. Freemotion 2

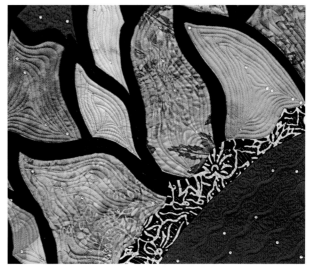

BLACK TIE GALA, detail of woven design. Full quilt on p. 35.

Fig. 6–5a.

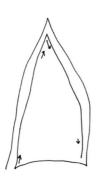

Fig. 6–5b.

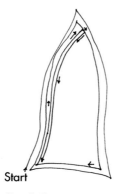

Fig. 6–5c.

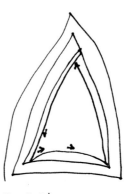

Fig. 6–5d.

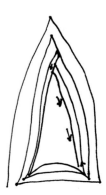

Fig. 6–5e.

Fig. 6–5f.

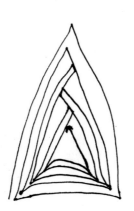

Fig. 6–5g.

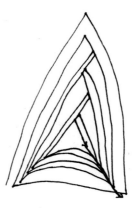

Fig. 6–5h.

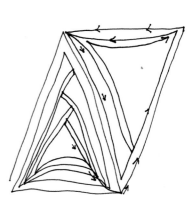

Fig. 6–5i.

Fig. 6–6a. Freemotion 3. TUSCANY MEMORIES, detail. Full quilt on p. 28.

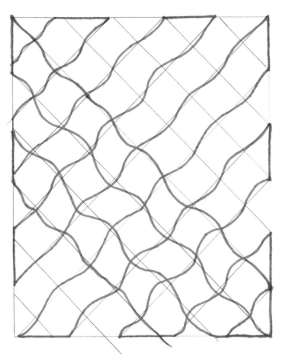

Fig. 6–6b. Freemotion 3. Pre-mark the grid and then freemotion quilt the curvy crosshatching.

Fig. 6–7. Freemotion 4. Start with the four skinny veins inside and then outline with curvy waves all around each vein.

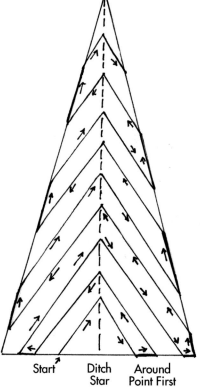

Start   Ditch   Around
        Star   Point First

Fig. 6–8. Freemotion 5

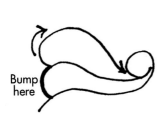

Bump here

Fig. 6–9a. Freemotion 6

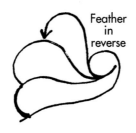

Feather in reverse

Fig. 6–9b.

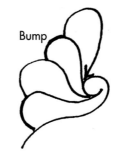

Bump

Fig. 6–9c.

Continue to swing around center circle

Fig. 6–9d.

Back to entry line

Fig. 6–9e.

1st feather in reverse to entry line

Fig. 6–9f.

Fig. 6–9g. Close up of Mary Sue Suit's original quilt PANSIES, quilted by author.

Fig. 6–10a. Freemotion 7 quilted sample

Fig.6–10b. Freemotion 7

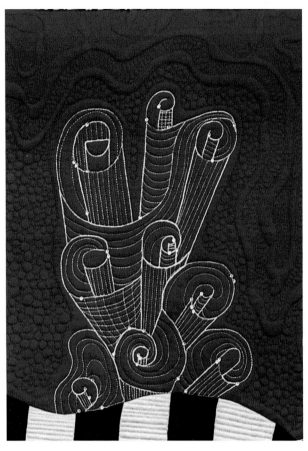

Fig. 6–11. BLACK TIE GALA, detail, sound waves close up. Full quilt on p. 35.

Fig. 6–12. BLACK TIE GALA, detail of back. Full quilt on p. 35.

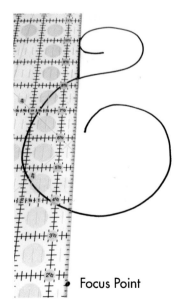

Focus Point

Fig. 6–13a. Ribbon step 1

I first learned how to do ribbon drawings from my daughter who learned how to draw them in art class. I loved drawing them. I've even seen some people piece or appliqué with the ribbons. Cara Gulati has a wonderful book on how to piece and appliqué these ribbons. I decided I would like to see if I could incorporate them into quilting. You can draw the pattern ahead of time and transfer to fabric or do what I did in BLACK TIE GALA. Draw the main lines and design in with a chalk pencil and then freemotion quilt the innards of the design (figs. 6–13a through 6–13j).

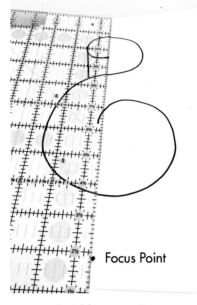

Fig. 6–13b. Ribbon step 2

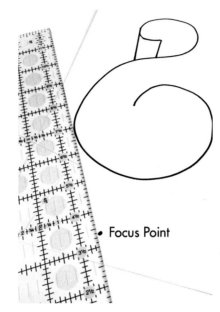

Fig. 6–13c. Ribbon step 3

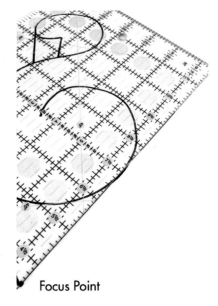

Fig. 6–13d. Ribbon step 4

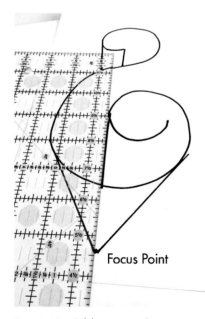

Fig. 6–13e. Ribbon step 5

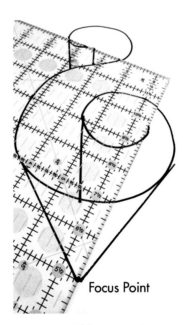

Fig. 6–13f. Ribbon step 6

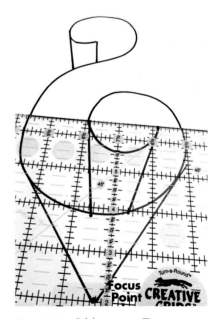

Fig. 6–13g. Ribbon step 7

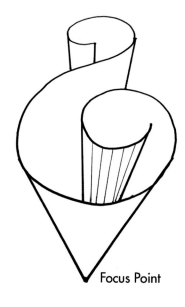

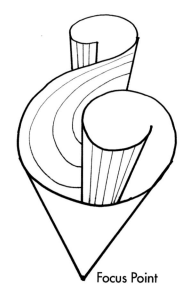

Fig. 6–13h. Ribbon step 8   Fig. 6–13i. Ribbon step 9   Fig. 6–13j. Ribbon step 10

When I quilt the main design I use rulers designed for the longarm to keep a straight line and sometimes quilt over these main lines several times, but when I do any of the curved lines, I do it without a ruler. It's smoother when you quilt this way.

Fig. 6–14a. Quilted sample

Fig. 6–14b. Author's original

Fig. 6–15a. Quilted sample

Fig. 6–15b. Author's original

Fig. 6–16a. Quilted sample

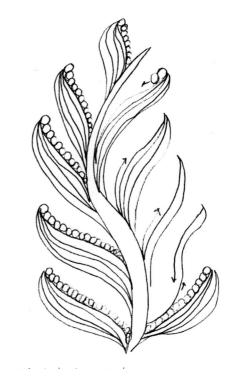

Fig. 6–16b. Author's original

Fig. 6–17a. Quilted sample

Fig. 6–17b. Author's original

Fig. 6–18a. Quilted sample

Fig. 6–18b. Author's original

Fig. 6–19a. Author's original

Fig. 6–19b. Quilted sample

Fig. 6–20a. Author's original

Fig. 6–20b. Quilted sample

Fig. 6–21a. Quilted sample

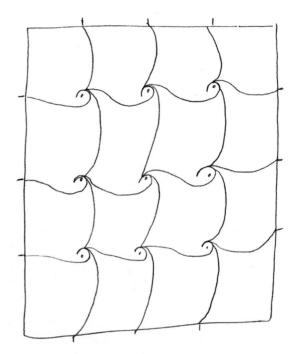

Fig. 6–21b. Author's original

Fig. 6–22a. Quilted sample

Fig. 6–22b. Author's original

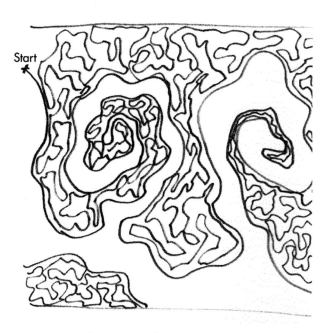

Fig. 6–23a. Author's original

Fig. 6–23b. Quilted sample

Fig. 6–24a. Author's original

Fig. 6–24b. Quilted sample

NEW QUILTING PATTERNS

Most of my quilting patterns start with a ⅛ drawing. You have to have a perfect half square triangle or it will not work. In my last book, *Make Your Own Quilting Designs & Patterns,* I go into this in quite some detail. To give you a very short review, either make a perfect square in your computer and draw a line from one corner to the opposite corner and that is your perfect triangle. Or if you have a square ruler, measure out and draw a 7½" square. Take your ruler and draw from one corner to the next as shown in fig. 7–1. Do the size at 7½" so that you can copy it in your computer. That way after you print your first design you can reverse the ⅛ drawing in any drawing or most photo programs so that you can tape these together to form a perfect ¼ drawing. The ¼ drawing you can copy four times and tape together to make your pattern. If it is not a perfect ⅛ or ¼ the design will never fit together to make your full drawing.

In these patterns I have shown you how I drew the initial ⅛ or ¼, or even in a few instances a ½ drawing. You can take the ¼ drawing and have 4 copies made at your copy center to resize the pattern so that it will fit on your quilt.

If you study how I drew the ⅛ or ¼ drawing it will give you some insight into how you can draw your own patterns and create your own designs. It helps to have a two-sided mirror. You can make one yourself if you go buy two flat mirrors and tape them together in the center with duct tape. That way you can see what the drawing looks like as you are progressing.

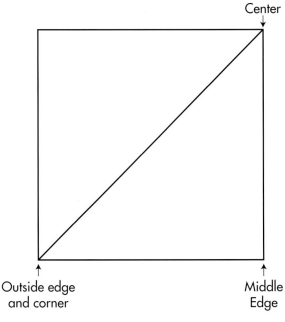

Fig. 7–1.

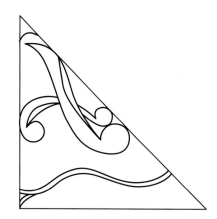

THE ART OF Quilting ♥ Judy Woodworth

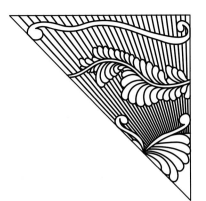

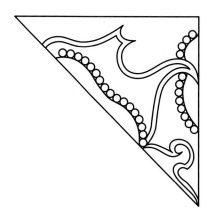

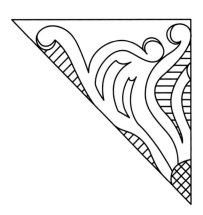

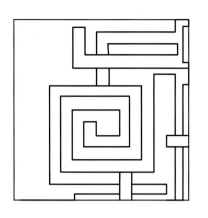
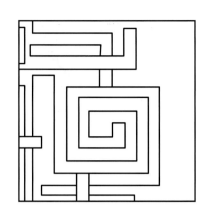

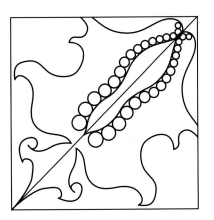

RESOURCES

GLIDE QUILT, 52" x 60". Designed and quilted by the author.

Mary Sue Suit   www.msquilt.com

Fil-Tec Bobbin Central (Glide Thread)   www.bobbincentral.com

Dover Publishing   www.Store.doverpublications.com

Blue Line Eraser   www.bluelineerasser.com

A Painter's Guide to Design and Composition by Margot Schulzke

Design & Composition Secrets of Professional Artists by
      International Artist

The Visual Dance by Joan Wolfrom   www.joanwolfrom.com

Color and Composition for the Creative Quilter — Katie Pasquini
      Masopust   www.katiepm.com

Design & Composition- Donna Baspaly   www.artists.ca/dbaspaly

Steven Aimone Design   www.aimoneartservices.com

Barbara Olson's Journey of an Art Quilter
      www.barbaraolsonquiltart.com

Lyric Kennard Quilting art magazine #23 and Art + Quilt Design
      Principles and Creativity Exercises   www.Lyrickinard.com

3-D Explosion- Cara Gulati   www.doodlepress.com

ABOUT THE AUTHOR

Judy is an International Award winning quilter, and author. Her books, *Freemotion Quilting, Make Your Own Quilting Designs & Patterns,* and now her current one *The Art of Quilting: Machine Techniques & Designs* were published with The American Quilter's Society. In 2012 she was the winner of the Paducah QuiltWeek® Best Longarm Quilter Award. She has been nominated three times as Best Machine Quilting Teacher and in 2014, she was named Best Machine Quilting Teacher at MQX.

She has written many articles published in professional machine quilter's magazines including: *On Track, Machine Quilting Unlimited, The Quilt Life,* and *AQ magazine.* In March of 2013, she was honored on the cover of *Machine Quilting Unlimited* as their featured quilter.

Judy has been featured on Linda Taylor's Longarm quilting show called *The Quilting School,* Alex Anderson and Ricky Tim's *The Quilt Show,* and Jodie Davis's *Quilt It: The Long Arm Quilting Show.*

Some of her most exciting quilting awards were winning first place twice at the International Quilt Show in Houston. Judy has won many awards at the American Quilter's Society shows, including Best Longarm Quilter, multiple awards at the Machine Quilter's Expo, and several dozen awards at the International Machine Quilting Showcase. She's also received a hundred other awards including Best of Show at the Nebraska State Fair which displayed over 700 quilts.

Judy has been married to her high school sweetheart for almost fifty years. He helps her paint many of her quilts. Her five children and eleven grandchildren have all been her biggest supporters in her quilting career.

Photo by: Bill Woodworth

MORE AQS BOOKS

This is only a small selection of the books available from the American Quilter's Society. AQS books are known worldwide for timely topics, clear writing, beautiful color photos, and accurate illustrations and patterns. The following books are available from your local bookseller, quilt shop, or public library.

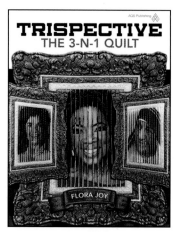

#10281

#10272

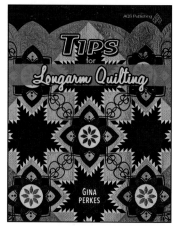

#10285

#10757

#10279

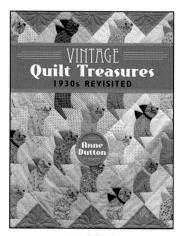

#10277

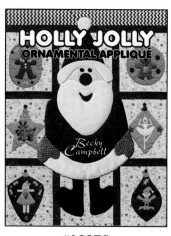

#10275

#10283

#10280